John
Children's Leader Guide

John
The Gospel of Light and Life

John: The Gospel of Light and Life
978-1-501-80533-2
978-1-501-80534-9 *eBook*

John: Large Print Edition
978-1-501-80535-6

John: Leader Guide
978-1-501-80536-3
978-1-501-80537-0 *eBook*

John: DVD
978-1-501-80541-7

John: Youth Study Book
978-1-501-80548-6
978-1-5018-0549-3 *eBook*

John: Children's Leader Guide
978-1-501-80550-9

For more information, visit www.AdamHamilton.org.

Also by Adam Hamilton

24 Hours That Changed the World

Christianity and World Religions

Christianity's Family Tree

Confronting the Controversies

Enough

Final Words from the Cross

Forgiveness

Leading Beyond the Walls

Love to Stay

Making Sense of the Bible

Not a Silent Night

Revival

Seeing Gray in a World of Black and White

Selling Swimsuits in the Arctic

Speaking Well

The Call

The Journey

The Way

Unleashing the Word

When Christians Get It Wrong

Why?

ADAM HAMILTON

Author of *The Way, The Journey,* and *24 Hours That Changed the World*

JOHN
The Gospel of Light and Life

Children's Leader Guide
by Susan Groseclose

Abingdon Press

Nashville

John
The Gospel of Light and Life

Children's Leader Guide
by Susan Groseclose

ISBN 978-1-5018-0550-9

15 16 17 18 19 20 21 22 23 24—10 9 8 7 6 5 4 3 2 1
MANUFACTURED IN THE UNITED STATES OF AMERICA

Contents

To the Leader

This children's leader guide is designed for use with Adam Hamilton's book and program *John: The Gospel of Light and Life*. This guide includes six lessons that follow the life of Jesus as it is presented in the Gospel of John. Children will learn about Jesus' life, death, and resurrection. They will learn who Jesus is and what it means to be a follower of Jesus Christ.

The subjects for each of the six lessons parallel the subjects in the program's adult and youth studies. Because of this feature, families will be able to discuss, across grade levels, what they have learned in each session.

The lessons in this guide, designed for children in kindergarten through sixth grade, are presented in a large group/small group format. Children begin with time spent at activity centers, followed by time together as a large group. Children end the lesson in small groups determined by grade level. Each lesson plan contains the following sections:

Focus for the Teacher

The information in this section will provide you with background information about the week's lesson. Use this section for your own study as you prepare.

Explore Interest Groups

In this section, you'll find ideas for a variety of activity centers. The activities will prepare the children to hear the Bible story. Allow the children to choose one or more of the activities that interest them. Occasionally there will be an activity that is recommended for all children, usually because it relates directly to a later activity. When this is the case, it will be noted.

Large Group

The children will come together as a large group to hear the scripture and story for the week. This section begins with a transition activity followed by the story and a Bible verse activity. A worship time concludes the large-group time.

Small Groups

Children are divided into grade level groups for small-group time. Depending on the size of your class, you may need to have more than one group for each grade level. It is recommended that each small group contain no more than twelve children.

Young Children
The activities in this section are designed for children in kindergarten through second grade.

Older Children
The activities in this section are designed for children in third through sixth grades.

Reproducible Pages

At the end of each lesson are reproducible pages, to be photocopied and handed out for all the children to use during that lesson's activities.

Schedule

Many churches have weeknight programs that include an evening meal, an intergenerational gathering time, and classes for children, youth, and adults. The following schedule illustrates one way to organize a weeknight program.

5:30	Meal
6:00	Intergenerational gathering introducing weekly themes and locations for the lesson. This time may include presentations, skits, music, and opening or closing prayers.
6:15–7:30	Classes for children, youth, and adults.

Churches may want to do this study as a Sunday school program. This setting would be similar to the weeknight setting. The following schedule takes into account a shorter class time, which is the norm for Sunday morning programs.

10 minutes	Intergenerational gathering
45 minutes	Classes for children, youth, and adults

Choose a schedule that works best for your congregation and its Christian education programs.

Blessings to you and the children as you learn about Jesus!

1 Jesus Is the Light

Objectives

The children will
- remember how God spoke and created the world.
- celebrate that God sent us his son, Jesus.
- discover what it means for Jesus to be the light for all people.
- explore ways to be children of the light.

Theme

God sent his son Jesus to be the light.

Bible Verse

The light for all people. (John 1:4)

Focus for the Teacher

Welcome to *John: The Gospel of Light and Life.* Over the next six weeks, we will discover and explore who Jesus is. Each week, children will hear and learn about a key Bible verse. They will explore and practice ways to live as followers of Jesus Christ.

This week, we learn that Jesus is the light for all people. In the beginning God spoke, and creation happened. In the Gospel of John, God who created the universe speaks to us by sending his son, Jesus.

Think of the song "This Little Light of Mine." The song teaches us that Jesus is the light and we are to shine that light. Children shine Jesus' light whenever they show Christ's love and care, such as when they befriend another child or when their family participates in a church mission project.

The song also teaches us not to hide Jesus' light. Children learn to shine Jesus' light even in those times when they experience the darkness. These dark times can be at the death of a grandparent or pet, when they experience teasing or bullying,

> We are children of the light.

or when they have problems in the home. It is in these dark times that Jesus offers us light, giving hope that we are not alone and that God is with us. Jesus' light shows us how to love and forgive one another. As the song says, we are not to hide the light. We are to shine our light for others. We are to be children of the light.

In this lesson we will be using light to remind children that Jesus is the light for all people. With younger children we will talk about ways to be children of the light. Older children will compare being children of the light and of the dark.

As you introduce children to Jesus as the light for all people, think about your own life. How have you experienced the light of Christ? How have these experiences deepened your understanding and trust in God? What has happened in your church or community that will illustrate for the children that Jesus is the light for all people?

Explore Interest Groups

Be sure that adult leaders are waiting when the first child arrives. Greet and welcome the children. Get the children involved in an activity that interests them and introduces the theme for the day's activities.

Jesus the Light

- **Say:** Today we are going to learn a Bible verse.

- Read the Bible verse, then recite it together: "The light for all people" (John 1:4).

- Give each child a copy of Reproducible 1a: Jesus the Light.

- Have children use crayons and colored pencils to decorate one or both of the light switch plates.

- Ask the children to cut out their light switch plates.

- **Say:** You can take this home and tape it to the light switch in your bedroom. Then, whenever you turn on the light, you can remember that Jesus is the light.

Sounds in the Dark

- Give each child a copy of Reproducible 1b: Sounds in the Dark.

- **Say:** The puzzle on this paper shows words that are sounds you might hear in the dark. The words may be written across, down, up, backward, or diagonally.

- **Ask:** Can you find all the hidden words?

- Encourage children to work the puzzle. When they are finished, have them share what they found.

- **Ask:** What other sounds might you hear in the dark? Do you like the dark? Why or why not?

- **Say:** We are going learn that Jesus shows us how to be children of the light and not children of the dark.

Prepare

- ✓ Make copies of **Reproducible 1a: Jesus the Light**, found at the end of the lesson, enough so each child can have one.

- ✓ Provide crayons, colored pencils, and scissors.

Prepare

- ✓ Make enough copies of **Reproducible 1b: Sounds in the Dark,** found at the end of the lesson, so there will be one for each child.

- ✓ Provide pencils.

Answer Key

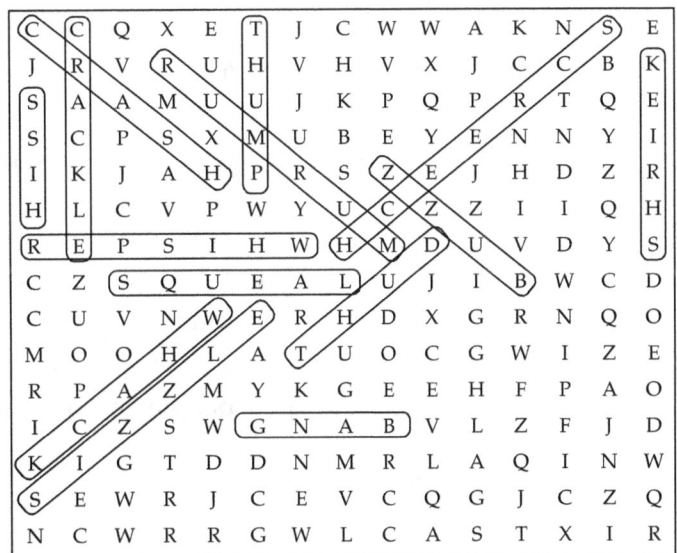

Prepare

✓ Provide toilet tissue rolls, small paper plates, yellow construction paper, crayons, markers, and glue.

Prepare

✓ Identify a large room or indoor area in which to play this game.

✓ Provide a flashlight.

Candle

- **Say:** Today we will be learning how Jesus is the light for all people and ways that we can be children of the light.

- Have each child color a toilet tissue roll and small paper plate.

- Glue the colored toilet tissue roll to the paper plate.

- Cut a flame from the yellow construction paper.

- Glue the flame to the top of the toilet tissue roll.

- **Say:** You can take your candle home and remember that Jesus is the light for all people.

I Am a Child of the Light

- **Ask:** When do you use a flashlight?

- **Say:** We are going to play a game with a flashlight. The light of the flashlight will find you in the dark, hidden areas of this room. When you are found, say: "Thank you, God. I am a child of the light."

- Invite one child to be "it." If you have a large group, you can choose two or three children.

- Cover the eyes of the child who is "it" and tell the child to count slowly to twenty while the other children in the group hide.

- Turn off the lights in the room.

- The child who is "it" uses the flashlight to find children's hiding spots.

- When the one who is "it" finds a child who is hidden, the child who is found says: "Thank you, God. I am a child of the light." Then that child can pair up with "it" to help find other children.

- Continue the game in this manner until all the children have been found.

- **Say:** Today we are going to learn how Jesus is the light for all people and how you can be a child of the light.

Large Group

Bring all the children together to experience the Bible story. Use a bell to alert the children to the large-group time.

God Spoke

- **Say:** In the beginning, God spoke and created the world.

- **Ask:** Where in the Bible do we read about God's creation?

- **Say:** We read about God's creation in the first book of the Bible, Genesis. Let's draw God's creation.

- Divide the children into six small groups. Pair younger children with older children.

- Give each group of children one of the newsprint sheets. If there are fewer than twelve children, the groups can work on more than one sheet.

- **Say:** Let us draw God's creation. On your group's sheet of paper draw what God created that day.

- As the groups finish their picture or pictures, hang their sheets on the wall, in order, to create a class mural. Hang the seventh sheet (God Rested) at the end of the mural.

- **Say:** God spoke and created the world.

Who Is Jesus?

- **Say:** God spoke and created the world. But even after God created the world, God wanted to speak to us. So God sent his son, Jesus.

- Invite a confident reader to read aloud John 1:1-2.

- **Say:** In the Gospel of John, we don't hear the familiar story of Jesus' birth. Instead we hear about the Word. John is telling us that God, who is the Word, sent his son Jesus. God wanted us to follow Jesus and learn how to live. Let's compare Jesus' life with your life.

- Give each child a copy of Reproducible 1c: Jesus and Me.

- Explain the worksheet, asking the children to think about the similarities and differences between Jesus' life and their own.

- Encourage the children to complete the worksheet and discuss it as you go through it together.

Prepare

✓ Provide seven sheets of newsprint (large sheets of paper). Each sheet will represent one day of creation. At the top of each sheet, put one of the following statements:
  o God spoke and created light so there was day and night.
  o God spoke and created the sky.
  o God spoke and created the earth and oceans.
  o God spoke and created the sun, stars, and moon.
  o God spoke and created the birds and fish.
  o God spoke and created all the animals and men and women.
  o God rested.

✓ Provide crayons and markers.

Prepare

✓ Provide each child with a copy of **Reproducible 1c: Jesus and Me,** found at the end of the lesson.

Prepare

✓ Write this week's Bible verse on a markerboard or piece of mural paper and place the verse where it can easily be seen. (The light for all people. John 1:4)

Prepare

✓ Provide a copy of "This Little Light of Mine" for each child, or write the words to the first verse and refrain on a markerboard at the front of the room.

✓ Get a glow stick for each child

The Light

• **Say:** Our Bible verse today will be easy to remember because it is only five words long!

• Invite the children to read the verse with you. Practice saying the verse several times.

• **Ask:** What does it mean for Jesus to be the light for all people?

• **Say:** Jesus was born so he could show us how to live. Jesus teaches us how to love others. Whenever we care for someone else or whenever we say "I'm sorry" or whenever we are kind to another person, we are sharing the light of Christ. We are being children of the light.

• Repeat the Bible verse together again.

Shine Your Light

• **Say:** God sent us his son, Jesus. Jesus is the light for all people. Let's learn a song together.

• Teach the children the first verse and refrain of "This Little Light of Mine."

• **Say:** We are to be children of the light. Jesus teaches us how to be children of the light.

• Give every child a glow stick and have them break it so their light shines.

• Turn off the lights in the room.

• **Say:** Jesus is the light for all people. Your glow stick shines in the darkness. When we follow Jesus we allow his light to shine. We become children of the light.

• Have children wave their glow sticks as you sing together "This Little Light of Mine."

• Dismiss children to their small groups.

Small Groups

Divide the children into small groups. You may organize the groups around grade levels or around readers and nonreaders. Keep the groups small, with a maximum of twelve children in each group. You may need to have more than one group of each grade level.

Young Children

- Have the children sit in a circle.

- **Say:** Let's review what we've learned today about Jesus.

- Encourage the children to share what they remember, asking questions to assist them if necessary.

- **Say:** We have learned that Jesus is the light for all people. We have also talked about ways that we can be children of the light. I'm going to read a sentence. If this is a child of the light, stand up. If not, stay in your seat.

- Read these statements one at a time and allow time for the children to respond.
  - o   You share your game with a friend.
  - o   You yell at your brother or sister.
  - o   You hug your mom or dad.
  - o   You see a student in your class being teased and join in teasing the student too.
  - o   You make a card for someone who is sick.
  - o   You say "I'm sorry" when you hurt another person.
  - o   You tell someone they are ugly.
  - o   You throw a candy wrapper on the ground.
  - o   You invite a new kid at school to play with you.
  - o   You tell your grandparent "I love you."

- If a statement is not being a child of the light, encourage the children to share ways they could be children of the light.

- **Ask:** What other ways might you be a child of the light?

- **Say:** This week, find ways that you can be children of the light.

- **Pray:** Thank you, God, for sending us your son Jesus to show us how to live. Thank you for showing us how Jesus is the light for all people. Show us how to be children of the light this week with our family and friends. Amen.

Prepare

✓ Create two signs: *Children of the Light* and *Children of the Dark.*

✓ Write each of the following words on an index card: *kind, greedy, loving, cruel, gentle, bickering, sharing, teasing, caring, hateful, forgiving.* Feel free to add other words that describe children of the dark and children of the light.

✓ Place the index cards facedown in a basket.

Older Children

- Have the children sit in a circle.

- **Ask:** What have you learned today about Jesus?

- Allow the children an opportunity to share, asking questions to prompt them as needed.

- On the floor or a table in the center of the circle, place the two signs: Children of the Light and Children of the Dark.

- **Say:** We are going to think about whether our actions are being children of the light or children of the dark. When we act as children of the light, we share Jesus' love. When we act as children of the dark, we hurt others.

- Pass the basket of cards around the circle and have the first child draw a card.

- Invite the child to read the card and place it on the appropriate sign.

- Take turns around the circle until the basket is empty.

- **Ask:** When have you been a child of the light?

- **Ask:** When have you experienced or seen someone acting hurtful?

- **Say:** When we experience cruelty or teasing, we can trust that Jesus is always with us. When we have been hurtful, we can ask God to forgive us and live differently.

- Pick up the cards on the sign Children of the Dark. Read the word on each card.

- **Ask:** How could you act differently from what this word describes, so you can be a child of the light rather than a child of the dark?

- Invite the children to stand in a circle and share one way each one plans to be a child of the light this next week.

- **Pray:** Thank you, God, for parents, teachers, and friends who encourage us. Help us be children of the light. Amen.

Jesus the Light

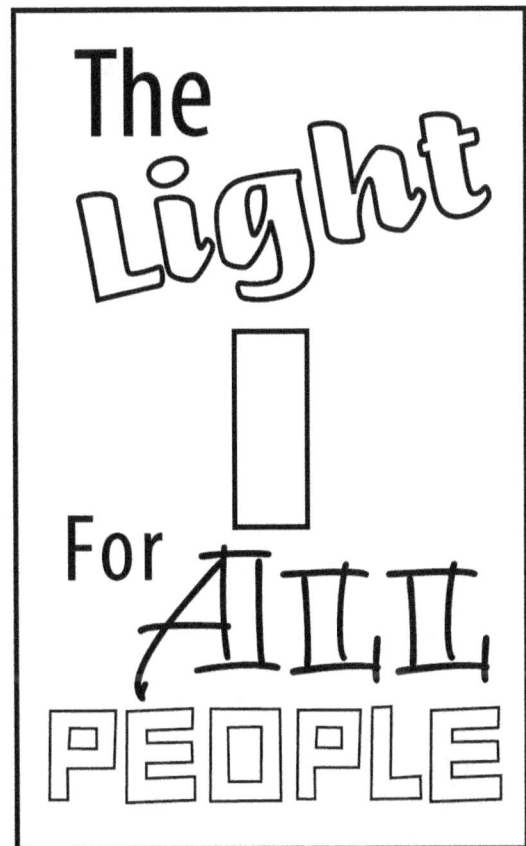

THE LIGHT FOR ALL PEOPLE

The Light For ALL PEOPLE

Sounds in the Dark

Find the words hidden in the puzzle. The words will be up, down, across, backward, or diagonal.

C	C	Q	X	E	T	J	C	W	W	A	K	N	S	E
J	R	V	R	U	H	V	H	V	X	J	C	C	B	K
S	A	A	M	U	U	J	K	P	Q	P	R	T	Q	E
S	C	P	S	X	M	U	B	E	Y	E	N	N	Y	I
I	K	J	A	H	P	R	S	Z	E	J	H	D	Z	R
H	L	C	V	P	W	Y	U	C	Z	Z	I	I	Q	H
R	E	P	S	I	H	W	H	M	D	U	V	D	Y	S
C	Z	S	Q	U	E	A	L	U	J	I	B	W	C	D
C	U	V	N	W	E	R	H	D	X	G	R	N	Q	O
M	O	O	H	L	A	T	U	O	C	G	W	I	Z	E
R	P	A	Z	M	Y	K	G	E	E	H	F	P	A	O
I	C	Z	S	W	G	N	A	B	V	L	Z	F	J	D
K	I	G	T	D	D	N	M	R	L	A	Q	I	N	W
S	E	W	R	J	C	E	V	C	Q	G	J	C	Z	Q
N	C	W	R	R	G	W	L	C	A	S	T	X	I	R

BANG	MURMUR	THUD
BUZZ	SCREECH	THUMP
CRACKLE	SHRIEK	WHACK
CRASH	SIZZLE	WHISPER
HISS	SQUEAL	

Jesus and Me

Read the facts below about Jesus' life. For each item, compare Jesus' life with your own. Is it the same or different? In each box, write or draw a picture showing how Jesus' life was the same as or different from yours.

Jesus was born in Bethlehem.

When Jesus was a baby, he slept in a manager.

Jesus' father, Joseph, was a carpenter.

Jesus grew up learning about God from his parents and the teachers in the Temple.

Jesus' mother was named Mary.

Jesus learned how to love, care for, and forgive others.

2 Jesus Cares

Objectives

The children will

- experience two Bible stories to learn how Jesus showed compassion.
- discover ways that children can be compassionate by caring for others.
- experience being a compassionate kid.

Theme

Jesus shows us how to care for one another.

Bible Verse

God's mighty works might be displayed in him. (John 9:3)

Focus for the Teacher

Today's lesson tells about two of the seven miracles, called "miraculous signs," which are found in the Gospel of John. The stories describing these miraculous signs show how Jesus cares for others and how children can be compassionate.

In John 2:1-12, Jesus was invited to a wedding party in Cana. The host had run out of wine, and Jesus helped him by changing the water into wine. This story takes a large amount of ordinary water and makes it extraordinary! We learn from the story that Jesus cares for all of us with extravagant love.

In John 9, Jesus opens the eyes of a man born blind. It happened when Jesus and his disciples saw a blind beggar on the side of the road. It was common in the first century for Jews to believe that being blind was a punishment for something that you did wrong. Jesus told the disciples that the man didn't sin; his blindness was so that "God's mighty works might be displayed in him" (John 9:3). It was an opportunity for Jesus to show his compassion.

Once Jesus healed the man, the Pharisees, who were religious leaders, became upset with Jesus.

> We are compassionate kids.

Jewish law forbade healing the sick on the Sabbath unless the person's life was in danger. They focused on the fact that Jesus broke the law rather than focusing on Jesus showing compassion by healing the man.

In these two stories, children can experience how Jesus showed compassion. At the wedding, he saved the host from being embarrassed. In the story of the blind man, Jesus saw the man and showed compassion by healing him.

Children do not understand the concept of spiritual blindness. However, they will understand that the disciples failed to see the man as a human being and that the Pharisees failed to see Jesus' care for the man.

As you discuss the Bible verse—"God's mighty works might be displayed in him" (John 9:3)— remind children that Jesus showed he cared. How have you experienced Jesus' care and compassion? What are some ways families in your congregation offer compassion to others?

Explore Interest Groups

Be sure that adult leaders are waiting when the first child arrives. Greet and welcome the children. Get the children involved in an activity that interests them and introduces the theme for the day's activities.

Squares of Compassion

This activity is recommended for all children, because it will be used in the large-group time.

- **Say:** Today we are going to make a paper quilt. Each one of you will decorate a quilt square, then we will put our squares together to make a quilt.

- Give each child a square of paper.

- **Ask:** What are some ways you can show that you care for others?

- **Say:** Each of you will write the word *care* somewhere on your quilt square and then decorate your square with a picture of how you can care for others.

- Encourage each child to write the word *care* on his or her square.

- Invite each child to decorate an individual quilt square.

- Have each child lay his or her square on the mural paper.

- Let the children arrange the squares.

- Have each child glue his or her square to the mural paper.

- Hang the quilt where others may enjoy it.

- **Say:** You took an ordinary square and made it into this extraordinary quilt! Today, we are going to hear a story of how Jesus took something ordinary and turned it into something extraordinary. We are also going to learn how Jesus calls us to be compassionate kids and to care for others.

I See

- **Say:** We are going to play a game to find out how observant you are.

- Choose a child to be the leader.

- The leader identifies an object in the room. The leader says, "I see something…(naming the color of the object)."

- The children look around the room and name different objects that are the correct color.

- The child who sees the correct object becomes the new leader.

- Continue the game in this manner.

- **Say:** We are going to hear a story today in which Jesus sees a man and shows care and compassion.

Prepare

- ✓ Provide mural paper, six-inch squares of paper, crayons, and glue.

- ✓ Cut a large piece of mural paper to serve as backing for a paper quilt.

- ✓ Lay the mural paper on a table or the floor.

Prepare

✓ Provide copies of **Reproducible 2a: Numbers! Numbers! Numbers!** found at the end of the lesson.

✓ Provide a calculator and pencils

✓ *Answer Key:* (1) 2 cups; (2) 4 cups; (3) 16 cups; (4) 320 cups; (5) 1,920 cups (6) "Amazing!" or "Awesome!" or any expression that the student chooses.

Prepare

✓ Provide a brownie mix, eggs, water, and oil

✓ Provide a "surprise" filling. This can be either maraschino cherries, chocolate kisses, or toffee pieces.

✓ Provide a pan for muffins.

✓ *Tip:* If you do not have time or access to an oven, make the brownies ahead of time and skip to arranging the brownies to serve.

Numbers! Numbers! Numbers!

- **Say:** Today we'll hear about how Jesus surprised everyone and turned water into wine. In the days of Jesus, water was often unsafe to drink, so people sometimes served wine instead of water. Let's find out how much water Jesus turned into wine.

- Give each child a copy of Reproducible 2a: Numbers! Numbers! Numbers!

- Encourage the children to complete the puzzle.

- **Say:** Jesus' compassion is overflowing!

Surprise Brownies

- **Say:** Today we'll hear a story about a wedding. Jesus had a surprise for people. We are going to make a surprise brownie for a snack.

- Prepare the brownies as directed on the mix.

- Pour a small amount of the brownie batter into each of the pan's greased muffin molds and spread smooth. Place the fillings onto the batter and push the "surprise" down into the batter slightly. Top with the remaining batter and gently spread smooth.

- *Tip:* Since brownies will not rise like cupcakes, you can fill the muffin molds slightly more than 2/3 full.

- Bake as directed on the package.

- Cool the brownies, then arrange them on a plate to serve during large-group time.

John: Children's Leader Guide

Large Group

Bring all the children together to experience the Bible story. Use a bell to alert the children to the large-group time.

Jesus Shows Compassion

- **Say:** Let's review what we learned about Jesus last week.
- Encourage children to share what they remember.
- **Say:** We learned that Jesus is the light for all people. One of the ways that Jesus is the light is to care for all people. Jesus teaches us how to be compassionate.
- **Say:** Today we are going to experience two stories in the Bible in which Jesus cared for others.
- Divide the class into two groups. Be sure you have a mix of younger and older children in each group. You will need at least one adult to work with each group.
- Give the members of one group copies of Reproducible 2b: Jesus' Surprise, and give the second group copies of Reproducible 2c: Jesus Opens the Man's Eyes.
- Encourage each group to choose their characters (listed at the top of the page) and briefly practice their parts. Feel free to add simple costumes and props.
- After a time of practice, bring the group back together.
- **Say:** Jesus has a surprise! Jesus was at a wedding party. Let's hear what happened.
- Invite the first group to share their story of Jesus' Surprise.
- **Say:** In another Bible story, Jesus showed his compassion to a man who was blind.
- Invite the second group to share the story of Jesus Opens the Man's Eyes.
- **Ask:** How did Jesus surprise the disciples and wedding guests?
- **Say:** Earlier some children in the group created a surprise.
- Have the children serve the surprise brownies.
- **Ask:** How did Jesus show compassion at the wedding?
- **Say:** Jesus saved the host from being embarrassed when he ran out of wine. In the Bible, water was used to wash hands rather than to drink. Jesus took a large amount of ordinary water and turned it into wine that people could drink. Jesus' care for us is beyond anything we can imagine!
- **Ask:** How did Jesus show compassion to the man who was blind?
- **Say:** In the Bible, "I see" means "I get it" or "I understand." The disciples and Pharisees saw the man as a beggar and sinner. Jesus saw him as a human being to be loved and healed. Jesus taught us that it's important to be compassionate to our family, our friends, and even to those we don't like.

Prepare

- ✓ Make copies of **Reproducible 2b: Jesus' Surprise** and **Reproducible 2c: Jesus Opens the Man's Eyes,** found at the end of the lesson.

- ✓ Provide the plate of surprise brownies (see Explore Interest Groups).

Prepare

✓ Provide sticky notes and markers.

✓ Write the word *compassion* on sticky notes, one letter per sticky note: C-O-M-P-A-S-S-I-O-N.

✓ Write the word *compassion* on a board or large sheet of paper for the children to see.

✓ *Tip*: If you have a large class, divide the children into groups of ten for this activity.

Compassion Scramble

- Place one sticky note on each child's back.

- **Say:** You each have a letter on your back. When I tell you to begin, you will need to work together to put yourselves in the correct order to spell the word compassion.

- Tell the children to begin. Encourage them to work together.

- Check to see if the children are in the right order.

- **Ask:** What does the word compassion mean? How do we care for others?

We Choose Compassion

- **Say:** As followers of Jesus, we are to be compassionate kids. We are to show others that we care. We are going to join together in a litany, where I say something and you answer. Your answer will be: We choose compassion! Jesus cares and I care!

- Have the children practice their response.

- Lead the children in the following litany, encouraging them to respond enthusiastically.
  - o Leader: When we wake up in the morning, we have a choice to make. We can grumble at our parents, or we can get up and get ready for the day.
  - o **All: We choose compassion! Jesus cares and I care!**
  - o Leader: The choices continue during the day. Will we always demand our own way, or will we consider the needs of others?
  - o **All: We choose compassion! Jesus cares and I care!**
  - o Leader: Will we say something mean or choose kind words?
  - o **All: We choose compassion! Jesus cares and I care!**
  - o Leader: If we see someone who is hurting or needs help, will we walk on by, or will we ask if we can help?
  - o **All: We choose compassion! Jesus cares and I care!**
  - o Leader: We remember that Jesus taught us how to care for others.
  - o **All: We choose compassion! Jesus cares and I care!**
  - o Leader: Amen.

- Dismiss children to their small groups.

Small Groups

Divide the children into small groups. You may organize the groups around grade levels or around readers and nonreaders. Keep the groups small, with a maximum of twelve children in each group. You may need to have more than one group of each grade level.

Young Children

- **Say:** Today, we have talked about how Jesus cares for others and how we can show compassion and care for others.

- **Ask:** What do you and your grandparents or older-adult friends talk about? What do you like to do with them? What words or pictures might bring a smile to them?

- **Say:** We are going to show our compassion to older persons in our community who are not able to come to church. We are going to create "Thinking of you" cards.

- Give each child a sheet of card stock paper.

- Tell the children to fold their paper in half, then fold it in half again to create a card.

- Encourage the children to write "Thinking of you" on the front and draw a picture using the colored pencils or crayons.

- Help the children write a message on the inside of their card and sign their name.

- As the children work on their cards, talk with them about ways that children care for others.

- **Say:** We will deliver these cards to older adults in our community. Thank you for showing your compassion. These cards will bring a smile to the adults who receive them.

- **Pray:** Compassionate Jesus, thank you for showing us how to love and be kind to others. Be with those who will receive our cards. May it remind them that you love them and that we care. Help us this week to be your compassionate kids by showing others that we care. Amen.

Prepare

- ✓ Provide white card stock paper, colored pencils, and crayons.

- ✓ *Optional*: Also provide stickers and templates of different shapes.

- ✓ *Tip*: Determine how to deliver cards to members in your congregation who are homebound or to an older-adult living facility in your community.

Prepare

✓ Provide a variety of snack items: peanut butter crackers, fruit cups and plastic spoons, power bars or granola bars, Vienna sausage, bottles of water. You will also need gallon-size re-sealable storage bags.

✓ *Tip*: You will need enough snack items so that children can fill two or three bags each. If you choose not to purchase the items, divide the list among the children. Send an e-mail to the parents telling them that their children will be making snack bags for the homeless. Ask them to provide a specific snack and indicate the specific number needed.

Older Children

- **Ask:** What does it look like to follow Jesus and be compassionate when you are at home? What does it look like at school? What does it look like at a sports event?

- Allow children an opportunity to share their ideas.

- **Ask:** Who remembers what Jesus did when he saw the man who was blind?

- **Say:** Remember that Jesus saw the man who was blind as a human being rather than as a sinner or a beggar.

- **Ask:** Who are some people we might not see as human beings?

- **Say:** Often, it can be hard to see people who are homeless as human beings. We often tend to think they are beggars. When we see them on the side of the road, it's easy to turn our heads, and sometimes we even lock our doors.

- **Say:** Today we're going to make snack bags for the homeless. You can keep these bags in your car, and when you see someone who is homeless you can give them a bag and tell them Jesus loves them.

- Have the children help put the snack items on the table in an assembly line.

- Give each child a gallon-size re-sealable bag.

- Have the children walk down the assembly line, filling their bag with each of the snack items.

- Repeat until all the bags are filled.

- Give the children several snack bags to take home. You may want to provide an information sheet telling the parents that the children are learning to show compassion. Ask the parents to keep the snack bags in the car and help the children hand them out to people who are homeless.

- *Optional*: Arrange for the group to deliver the snack bags to one of the community shelters for the homeless. Check in advance with the shelter and find out what they recommend.

- **Say:** This week when you see someone who is homeless, give them a snack bag and tell them Jesus loves them. I look forward to hearing your stories next week about showing compassion.

- Have the children form a circle. Invite them to share their joys and concerns for prayer time.

- **Pray:** Awesome God, thank you for hearing our prayers, even those we don't speak out loud. Today we pray for the joys and concerns we have mentioned. We thank you for Jesus Christ, who teaches us how to show compassion to others. We thank you for [name each child in the group]. Help us this week to be compassionate kids. Amen.

Numbers! Numbers! Numbers!

Each of these six big jars holds about 20 gallons of water. How much water is that?
Complete this puzzle to find out.

1. How many cups are in a pint? Write the correct number in this jar.

2. How many cups are in a quart? Write the correct number in this jar.

3. How many cups are in a gallon? Write the correct number in this jar.

4. If each jar holds 20 gallons of water, how many cups of water are in each jar? Write the correct number in this jar.

5. There are 6 jars. So, how many total cups of water do all the jars hold? Write the correct number in this jar.

6. Think of a word or phrase to describe Jesus' miracle of changing all those cups of water into wine. Write your word or phrase in the space below.

Jesus' Surprise

Speaking parts: Narrator, Mary, Jesus, Headwaiter
Nonspeaking parts: Disciples, Servants, Groom, Wedding Guests

Narrator: There was a wedding party in Cana of Galilee. Jesus and his disciples were there, and so was Mary, Jesus' mother. When the wine ran out, Mary turned to Jesus.

Mary: They don't have any wine. What should we do?

Jesus: Don't worry. I'll take care of it.

Narrator: Mary called the servants.

Mary: Do whatever Jesus tells you.

Narrator: Nearby were six stone water jars. The wedding guests would use water from the jars to wash their hands. Each jar was able to hold about twenty or thirty gallons of water.

Jesus: (To the servants) Fill the jars with water.

Narrator: The servants filled the jars to the brim.

Jesus: Now draw some water from them and take it to the headwaiter.

Narrator: The servants drew some water and took it to the headwaiter. The headwaiter tasted the water.

Headwaiter: This isn't water. It's wine! And not just any wine, but fine wine.

Narrator: This was the first miraculous sign that Jesus did in Cana of Galilee. He revealed his glory, and his disciples believed in him.

–Based on John 2:1-11

Jesus Opens the Man's Eyes

Speaking parts: Narrator, Disciple, Jesus, Man, Pharisee, Neighbor
Nonspeaking parts: Other Disciples, Other Pharisees, Other Neighbors

Narrator: As Jesus and his disciples walked along, they saw a man who had been blind since birth. In Jesus' day, people believed that if you were blind, it meant you had done something wrong and it was a punishment from God.

Disciple: (To Jesus) Rabbi, since the man was born blind, someone must have sinned or done something wrong. Did the man sin? Did his mother and father sin?

Jesus: The man and his parents didn't do anything wrong. The man is blind so that God's mighty works might be displayed in him.

Narrator: After Jesus spoke, he spit into the dusty ground, made mud, and smeared the mud on the man's eyes.

Jesus: (To the man) Go, wash in the pool of Siloam.

Narrator: So the man went away and washed. When he returned, he was jumping for joy.

Man: I can see! I can see!

Narrator: But Jesus had healed the man on the day of rest, called the Sabbath, which was against the religious law. The man's neighbors were upset, so they took the man to the religious leaders, who were called Pharisees.

Pharisee: We thought you were blind. How can you see?

Man: Jesus put mud on my eyes. He healed me.

Neighbor: Jesus broke the Sabbath law!

Man: All I know is that I was blind, and now I can see.

Narrator: It was a miraculous sign. By healing the man, Jesus was showing God's mighty works.

–Based on John 9

3 Jesus Brings Life

Objectives	Theme
The children will • explore the seven "I AM" sayings to understand how they describe Jesus. • learn how Jesus is the way, the truth, and the life. • discover how to be followers of the Way.	We learn to be followers of the Way by living like Jesus. **Bible Verse** I am the way, the truth, and the life. (John 14:6)

Focus for the Teacher

"I Am" is a name for God, told by God to Moses at the burning bush. In the Gospel of John, the seven "I AM" sayings link Jesus to God and give witness that Jesus is God's son. Each of the sayings describes a way in which Jesus gives light and life to those who believe.

We will focus on the saying, "I am the way, the truth, and the life" (John 14:6). Jesus is the way. He told his disciples in the upper room that he was going to prepare a place for them. Jesus promised that he would send the Holy Spirit to continue to show them the way.

As Christians, we believe that Jesus is our source of salvation. God sent us his son, Jesus, and through Jesus we are given eternal life. Our salvation is a gift from God, offered not just to professing Christians but to all people. It is through Jesus Christ that we know the way to live. It is through Jesus Christ that we have the truth of God's love and justice. It is through Jesus Christ that we are given eternal life.

The early Christians were called followers of "the Way." Just as children can understand the different names they have, such as daughter/son, friend, classmate, dancer, scout, and so forth, children can claim their identity as followers of the Way. Children can learn that whenever we share, whenever we love and care for others, whenever we forgive another person, we are following the Way.

> We are followers of the Way.

How have the children in your group shown that they can be followers of the Way? Older children can imagine or role-play different situations to help them decide to be followers of Jesus and of the Way.

For young children, it will be helpful to think of concrete ways in which they can be followers of the Way. These might include being kind to a child at school, doing a chore around the house, picking up trash, calling their grandparents, or making a card for someone who is sick.

Affirm the different ways in which both older and younger children have followed Jesus.

Explore Interest Groups

Be sure that adult leaders are waiting when the first child arrives. Greet and welcome the children. Get the children involved in an activity that interests them and introduces the theme for the day's activities.

I Am...

- Write across the mirror: I Am . . .

- **Say:** Today we are going to discover how we can follow Jesus. One of the ways that we follow Jesus is to pray. Look at your reflection and think about words that describe you.

- Have the children write on the mirror words that describe what they are like (loving, caring, creative, intelligent, fun).

- **Say:** We are all different, and we are all children of God. Thank God for who you are.

Prepare

- ✓ Set a floor-length mirror horizontal on a table.

- ✓ Provide washable fine-tip markers.

Following the Way

- Explain the route through the obstacle course to the children.

- Divide the children into pairs. Blindfold a child in each pair.

- **Say:** If you are blindfolded, you will need to trust and follow your leader to get you through the obstacle course safely.

- Invite the pairs of children to take turns going through the obstacle course.

- Encourage the children to swap being leader and being blindfolded and go back through the course.

- **Ask:** How did you feel being blindfolded? How did you feel being the leader?

- **Say:** Today, we are going to talk about Jesus being the way, the truth, and the life. We trust Jesus to lead us. When we follow Jesus, we are followers of the Way.

Prepare

- ✓ Create a short obstacle course using objects in the room. For example, you might set up several chairs that the children have to walk around, followed by a couple of hula hoops that have to be stepped in, followed by a table that must be crawled under, and so forth.

- ✓ Place a line of masking tape on the floor several feet in front of the first obstacle and several feet after the last obstacle to indicate the start and finish lines.

- ✓ Provide blindfolds.

Prepare

✓ Provide beading string, keychain rings, scissors, plastic beads, and a variety of letter beads.

✓ *Tip*: Check YouTube for a video to watch step-by-step directions.

Name Keychain

- **Say:** You have different names that describe who you are. For example, you are a grandson or granddaughter, a friend, a classmate, or a teammate.

- **Ask:** What are some names that describe you?

- **Say:** Jesus had many names that described him. Some of those names are light of the world or good shepherd or true vine. Today, we are going to create a name bracelet. When creating the bracelet, you may choose to use your name or a name that describes you.

- Have each child cut a length of string about two feet long.

- Have the children fold their string in half and put approximately one inch of the folded end of the string through the keychain ring.

- Have each child reach through the loop formed by the folded end of the string and pull both of the ends of the string through the loop, to secure the string to the ring.

- Give each child a set of letter beads to spell the name they have chosen.

- Encourage the children to string colored beads through both ends of the string.

- When four to six colored beads have been strung, add the alphabet beads to spell their name.

- String four to six more colored beads.

- When they finish beading or reach the end of the string, have each child tie the two ends of the string together into a knot.

- Trim off the extra string.

- **Say:** You can attach your keychain to your backpack or use it as a zipper pull on your jacket. Today, we are going to be learning about one of Jesus' names or descriptions: "I am the way, the truth, and the life."

Prepare

✓ Provide copies of **Reproducible 3a: Names of Jesus**, found at the end of the lesson.

Names of Jesus

- **Say:** Today we are going to learn more about Jesus. You have many different names that describe you, such as son, daughter, dancer, or soccer player. These names describe how you are related to others or what you do in your life.

- **Ask:** What are some of the names that describe you?

- **Say:** In the Gospel of John, Jesus has seven "I AM" sayings. These sayings tell us about different names for Jesus and ways to describe Jesus.

- Give each child a copy of Reproducible 3a: Names of Jesus.

- **Say:** Unscramble the words to discover the different "I AM" sayings of Jesus. You can read the clues and look up the Bible verses to help you unscramble the words.

Large Group

Bring all the children together to experience the Bible story. Use a bell to alert the children to the large-group time.

Jesus Is Like That and More!

- **Say:** I have hidden word cards around the room that describe Jesus.
- Encourage the children to find a word card.
- When they find one word card, they will bring it back to their seat. Wait for everyone to find a word card and sit down.
- **Ask:** Look at your word card. How is Jesus like this?
- Invite each child to share the word on the card and tell how Jesus is like that.
- After each child shares, encourage the children to respond, "Jesus is like that and more!"

Jesus Is the Way

- **Ask:** Whom have we been learning about? What have we learned about Jesus so far?
- Encourage the children to review what they have learned.
- **Ask:** Think about your own name. Do you know who you were named after?
- Encourage children to share stories about their names.
- **Say:** In the Gospel of John, Jesus says: I am the light, I am the good shepherd, I am the bread of life. These are different ways to describe Jesus. Today we are going to learn how Jesus is the way, the truth, and the life.
- Show each navigational tool.
- **Ask:** When we want to get someplace, how does this show us the way?
- Encourage children to share their ideas for each navigational tool.
- **Ask:** Who do you ask for advice? Whose instructions do you follow?
- **Say:** When we follow our parents, grandparents, and teachers, we trust that they know the way. They will give us good advice. They will tell us what to do or what not to do. They will protect us and keep us safe.
- **Ask:** How is Jesus the way?
- **Say:** Jesus knows the way we should live. As we read Bible stories about Jesus, we learn how to be loving, caring, and forgiving.

Prepare

- ✓ Use index cards to create word cards. Write one word on each card that describes Jesus: loving, caring, forgiving, courageous, heals, teaches, compassionate, sharing, providing, righteous, mighty, kind, and so forth.
- ✓ *Tip*: Provide a word card for each child. You can create two or three cards using the same word.

Prepare

- ✓ Provide a map, GPS, compass, globe, or other navigational tools

Prepare

✓ Write this week's Bible verse on a markerboard or a piece of mural paper and place it where it can easily be seen. (I am the way, the truth, and the life. John 14:6)

Prepare

✓ Write the letters of the word *Christian* vertically on a markerboard or piece of mural paper.

✓ Check out YouTube for a version of the song *I Am a C-H-R-I-S-T-I-A-N* and arrange for a way to show the video to the children.

Bible Verse Chant

• Show the children the Bible verse. Encourage them to read the Bible verse with you.

• Add motions to the words. Squat down when you say "I am the way"; stand up when you say "the truth"; raise your arms overhead when you say "and the life. "

• Divide the class into four groups, giving each a number, Group 1 through Group 4.

• **Say:** We are going to divide our verse into three parts. We'll work together to say the verse. Group 1 will say the first phrase, Group 2 will say the second phrase, and Group 3 will say the third phrase. Group 4 will then begin again and say the first phrase, then we'll go back to Group 1 to say the second phrase. We'll continue that way until we've said the verse four times and each group has had a chance to begin the verse. As you say your group says it's part of the phrase, perform the motion that goes along with that part of the phrase. You'll need to pay attention to know when your group is supposed to talk, what you are supposed to say, and what motin to make!

• Encourage the class to say the Bible verse four times as directed.

• **Say:** This verse reminds us that Jesus shows us how to live. We can be followers of the Way.

Followers of the Way

• **Say:** When we follow Jesus and live as followers of the Way, we are given a new name. We are *Christians*.

• Show the video *I Am a C-H-R-I-S-T-I-A-N* and encourage the children to sing along.

• **Say:** Does everyone know what an acrostic is? We make an acrostic by writing the letters on a sheet of paper, then filling in a word that starts with each of the letters.

• Show the children the markerboard or mural paper with the word *Christian* written vertically.

• **Say:** We are going to create an acrostic prayer to show the different ways we can be a Christian, showing that we can be followers of the Way.

• Encourage the children to identify a word that begins with each letter in the word *Christian* that describes how they can follow Jesus. Write the word on the acrostic.

• **Pray**: Thank you, Jesus, for showing us how to live. Help us be followers of the Way. Help us be a faithful Christian as we are . . . (Invite the children to read the words in the acrostic prayer.)

• Dismiss children to their small groups.

Small Groups

Divide the children into small groups. You may organize the groups around grade levels or around readers and nonreaders. Keep the groups small, with a maximum of twelve children in each group. You may need to have more than one group of each grade level.

Young Children

- **Say:** Today we've talked about being followers of the Way. When we love others, care for others, forgive others, and share, we are following Jesus. We are being followers of the Way. Today we are going to make followers of the Way sandals.

- Give each child a piece of white card stock paper big enough for two footprints.

- Divide the group into pairs.

- Encourage the children to work together to trace both of each other's feet.

- Cut out the feet to make paper sandals.

- Come back to the group. Invite the children to write words or draw pictures on their sandals showing the ways they will follow Jesus this week.

- Have the children punch a hole on each side of their sandals near the ball of the foot, then punch a hole in the center near the top of the foot.

- Have them cut two short pieces of chenille stem, then thread two or three big buttons on each chenille stem.

- Thread one chenille stem from the hole on the ball of the foot to the hole on the top of the foot to create a strap.

- Fasten the strap with tape on the bottom of the sandal.

- Repeat on the other side.

- **Ask:** How are you going to follow Jesus this week?

- **Say:** You can take your sandals home. Whenever you see them, remember how you can be followers of the Way.

- **Pray:** Jesus, thank you for showing us how to live. Help us to share your love and care with everyone we meet. Help us to be followers of the Way. Amen.

✓ Provide white card stock paper, pencils, scissors, crayons, colored pencils, hole punch, chenille stems, big buttons, and tape.

✓ *Optional*: Tape footprints with the Bible verse on the floor from the large group to the small group. Cut out nine footprints and write one word of the Bible verse on each footprint. (I am the way, the truth, and the life.)

Prepare

✓ Copy **Reproducible 3b: Role Play Scenarios,** found at the end of the lesson. Cut out each scenario, fold, and place in a basket.

✓ Provide index cards and pens.

Older Children

- **Say:** Last week we made snack bags for people who are homeless.

- **Ask:** What happened when you gave a person one of the snack bags?

- Encourage the children to share their stories.

- **Say:** When you show others that you care, you not only are a compassionate kid but you also are a follower of the Way. You act like Jesus would. As followers of the Way, we rely on Jesus to help us make decisions about what we believe and how we treat others.

- **Ask:** When is it hard to be a follower of the Way? When is it easy to be a follower of the Way?

- **Say:** We are going to roleplay some situations and think about how we can be followers of the Way.

- Divide the group into pairs. Each pair picks a scenario from the basket.

- Encourage the pair to act out the situation for the group and show how they can be followers of the Way.

- **Say:** The decisions we make in our relationships and the way we live each day show others that we are followers of the Way. Our parents, teachers, and friends help us be followers of the Way.

- **Ask:** What are some ways they can help us?

- Give each child an index card and pen. Have them write the names of three people they can count on to help them remember to be a follower of the Way.

- **Say:** This week, do your best to be a follower of the Way. If you find yourself in a situation and don't know what to do, talk with one of the people on your card and then together figure out how to be a follower of the Way.

- **Pray:** God, thank you for adults and friends who encourage us. Help us to be faithful followers of the Way. Help us to show others that you are the way, the truth, and the life. Amen.

Names of Jesus

Using the clues provided, unscramble the word to discover the "I AM" sayings, then write the unscrambled word in the blank space. If you can't guess the word from the clues, you can look up the Bible verse.

I am the deabr _____ of life. (John 6:35)

  We eat this when we take Communion to remember that Jesus is love.

I am the gtilh _____ of the world. (John 8:12)

  We are to shine Jesus' love.

I am the gate of the hepse _____. (John 10:7; also verse 9)

  Jesus takes care of us just like shepherds care for these animals.

I am the odgo _____ shepherd. (John 10:11,14)

  The kind of shepherd Jesus is—the opposite of bad.

I am the csueritrrnoe _____ and the life. (John 11:25)

  What it was called when Jesus rose from the dead.

I am the ayw _____, the truth, and the life. (John 14:6)

  The path that the early Christians followed.

I am the uert _____ vine. (John 15:1; also verse 5)

  The kind of help Jesus gives us, which is the opposite of false.

Roleplay Scenarios

Your older brother yells at you when you walk into his room without knocking. What do you do?

— —

You are playing volleyball and you hit the ball near the out-of-bounds line. The other team says that the ball was out-of-bounds, but you think it may have been inbounds. What do you do?

— —

You open up a Christmas gift from your grandmother, but it isn't something you wanted. What do you do?

— —

You are leaving gym class and notice a group of kids teasing and bullying a classmate. He is crying and asking for his gym bag back. What do you do?

— —

You and a friend are walking home from school. You notice that your friend throws her gum wrapper on the ground. What do you do?

— —

You see one of your friends point to a classmate and say, "She's ugly." What do you do?

— —

You're walking down the hallway, and a teacher you don't like walks past you. The teacher accidently drops her books and papers all over the floor. What do you do?

— —

You and some friends are playing soccer in the park. You notice that someone your age is on the sideline watching. What do you do?

— —

Your mother has had a hard day at work and is tired. After dinner you ask her to play a game with you, but she says that first she has to load the dishwasher, take out the trash, fold the clothes in the dryer, and make sure your younger sister takes a bath. What do you do?

I am the way, the truth, and the life. (John 14:6)

4 Jesus' Final Instructions

<table>
<tr><td>

Objectives

The children will
- explore Jesus' last instructions to the disciples.
- experience ways to stay in love with God.
- experience ways to love and serve others.

</td><td>

Theme

Jesus left us instructions to love God and to serve others.

Bible Verse

Remain in my love. (John 15:9b)

</td></tr>
</table>

Focus for the Teacher

In the Gospel of John, Jesus leaves four instructions to his disciples the last night they were together in the upper room. These instructions include:

- Jesus is always with us. The Holy Spirit comforts and guides our lives.

- We are to remain connected to Jesus Christ. This instruction is part of the last "I AM" saying, "I am the true vine" (John 15:1). Just as a branch can only live and bear fruit if it remains connected to the vine, we live and bear fruit by staying connected to Jesus Christ, the true vine. We stay in love with Christ through Bible study and reflection, prayer, and worship.

- We are to obey Jesus' command to love. As we stay connected to the vine, Jesus Christ, we bear fruit. Jesus tells the disciples that to be fruit is to follow his commands to "love each other just as I have loved you. Love is not a feeling but rather the way we act as we selflessly serve and care for others, support and advocate for others, and build up one another and the community.

> We are servants of Christ, loving God and others.

- We are to serve others just as Jesus served his disciples when he washed their feet.

Children are familiar with instructions from their parents, teachers, coaches, and other important adults in their lives. The instructions that Jesus gave to his disciples can be summarized in the Great Commandment to love God and love neighbor. Loving God means staying connected to Jesus Christ and living with the assurance that the Holy Spirit is always with us. Loving your neighbor means loving and serving others.

Spend time this week thinking about your own relationship with Jesus Christ. What spiritual practices help you stay in love with God? What are ways that the Holy Spirit has comforted, led, guided, and empowered you? Name times in your daily or weekly life when you love and serve others. Can you recall a time when loving or serving others has been especially difficult or easy?

Explore Interest Groups

Be sure that adult leaders are waiting when the first child arrives. Greet and welcome the children. Get the children involved in an activity that interests them and introduces the theme for the day's activities.

Instructions from the Heart

- **Say:** Right before Jesus died, he gave some final instructions to his disciples. He told his disciples to love God and love others.

- **Ask:** What are some ways you can love God? What are some ways you can love others?

- Give each child a square sheet of paper and Reproducible 4a: Instructions from the Heart.

- Have the children follow the directions on the reproducible.

- **Say:** Take your heart home and remember Jesus' instructions to love God and love others.

Prepare

- ✓ Provide copies of **Reproducible 4a: A Fun Way to Fold a Message,** found at the end of this lesson.

- ✓ Write on markerboard or a piece of mural paper: *Love God and love others.*

- ✓ Provide 8"x8" square pieces of paper, pencils, pens, crayons, and markers.

- ✓ *Tip:* Before the session, practice folding a heart message so that you can help the children with this task. You may want to check out YouTube for visual instructions on how to fold an easy origami heart.

Prayer Cards

- **Say:** We are to stay in love with Jesus Christ. One of the ways that we stay in love is to pray. We can pray anytime and anywhere. We can pray about anything. We can thank God for a beautiful sunset or ask God to be with people who might be hurt. Today we are going to make some prayer reminders.

- Give each child several index cards.

- Have each child write the word "PRAY" in large letters on each card.

- Encourage the children to decorate their cards.

- **Say:** When you take these cards home, put them around your house in places where you will see them frequently. When you see a card, take a moment and say a prayer. The prayer doesn't need to be long or complicated. It can be as simple as "God, thank you for this day." Remember we can pray about anything!

Prepare

- ✓ Provide index cards, markers, and crayons.

Prepare

✓ Arrange a circle of chairs facing inward, using one chair fewer than the number of children in your class.

Doing Good Things

- **Say**: We have many opportunities to love and serve others every day. We are going to play a game about doing good things for other people.

- Choose one child to stand in the center of the circle of chairs, and have the rest of the children sit in the chairs.

- Explain the following rules to the children:

- The person in the center will say a good thing they have done for someone else, such as "I made a get-well card for someone" or "I gave clothes that don't fit me anymore to someone else" or "I read a book to my younger sister."

- Every person in the circle for whom that statement is true must get up and find a new seat, while the person in the middle tries to get a seat also.

- The person left standing becomes the next person to tell a good thing they have done.

- Encourage the children to play the game.

- **Say**: You have done many good things!

Prepare

✓ Provide red and pink construction paper, scissors, and markers.

✓ *Tip*: Cut the construction paper into different size squares that can be cut into hearts by the children.

✓ Plan a route for the children through the church building, getting permissions where necessary.

Love Notes

- **Ask**: Do you like fun surprises?

- **Say**: Today we're going to make some surprise messages for other people in our church.

- Have the children cut out a lot of hearts in a variety of sizes from the construction paper.

- Encourage the children to work together and write on each heart, "God loves you" or "You are loved."

- When all the hearts have a message on them, ask the children to go with you through the church building to distribute the hearts where people will find them. You might suggest that they put hearts on some of the seats in the sanctuary or in some of the hymnals. If your church has mailboxes for staff or members, you might put hearts in the mailboxes.

- **Ask**: How do you think people will feel when they discover a surprise heart? How does it make you feel to leave these surprises?

- **Say**: God's love is for everyone. Thank you for making reminders of God's love.

Large Group

Bring all the children together to experience the Bible story. Use a bell to alert the children to the large-group time.

Useful to Serve Others

- Show the children all the items you have gathered.
- **Say:** All these items have something in common. Everything here can be used to love and serve others.
- Pick up one item at a time and show it to the children.
- **Ask:** How do you think this item could be used to love and serve others?
- Allow the children to share their ideas about each item. Encourage them to think of many options for each item.
- **Say:** As you can see, there are many different ways to love and serve others.

Jesus Shows Us How to Live

- Invite the children to sit at tables.
- **Ask:** What have we learned about Jesus so far?
- Encourage the children to review what they have learned.
- **Say:** Jesus gave his disciples four instructions on the last night he was with them in the upper room. These are instructions for us too.
- **Ask:** What instructions do your parents give you? What kinds of instructions do you think Jesus gave to his disciples and to us?
- Give each child a copy of Reproducible 4b: Instructions from Jesus.
- **Say:** First, Jesus told the disciples that even though he was going to die, he would always be with them in their hearts. Jesus will always love us and show us the way.
- **Ask:** How do we know that Jesus will always be with us?
- Encourage children to write or draw their thoughts in the space provided. Invite children to share their ideas.
- **Say:** Second, Jesus told the disciples to stay in love with God.
- **Ask:** What are some ways we can stay in love with God?
- Encourage children to write or draw their thoughts in the space provided. Invite children to share their ideas.
- **Say:** Third, Jesus told his disciples to love others. Love isn't just a feeling. It is a way that we care for others and a way we stand up for others.
- **Ask:** What are some ways we can love others?

Prepare

✓ Provide a variety of items useful in serving others, such as a soup pot, telephone, shovel, coat, offering plate, chalice, musical instrument, adhesive bandage, coffee cup, bread, envelope, and so forth.

Prepare

✓ Provide copies of **Reproducible 4b: Instructions from Jesus,** found at the end of this lesson.

✓ Provide pencils, bottles of hand sanitizer, and Bibles.

- Encourage children to write or draw their thoughts in the space provided. Invite children to share their ideas.
- **Say:** Finally, Jesus didn't just tell the disciples to love others; he showed them how to serve others.
- Have the children sit in groups of four or six.
- Give a child in each group a bottle of hand sanitizer.
- Encourage the child to wash their neighbor's hands.
- Tell the child to pass the bottle of hand sanitizer to their neighbor.
- Continue around the circle till everyone has had a chance to wash another's hands.
- Invite the children to turn to John 13 in their Bibles. Older children can help younger children.
- Invite a confident reader to read John 13:4-5 and another child to read John 13:12-14.
- **Say:** In Jesus' days, people wore sandals. After walking all day, the disciples' feet were dusty and dirty. Usually a servant washed the guest's feet. However, this time Jesus washed the disciples' feet. They couldn't imagine that Jesus, their leader, would wash their feet. We are to serve others just as Jesus served his disciples by washing their feet.
- **Ask:** What are some ways we can serve others?
- Encourage children to write or draw their thoughts in the space provided. Invite children to share their ideas

Prepare

✓ If you are not familiar with the hymn "Jesu, Jesu, Fill Us With Your Love," you can find it in many hymnals or online. You may also want to listen to the melody online.

✓ Provide a way for the children to access the words of the hymn.

Love Leads to Serving

- **Say:** When we stay in love with Jesus, we want to share God's love. We want to serve others.

- **Ask:** What are some ways you serve at home? At school? At church?

- **Say:** Today we are going to learn a hymn that reminds us to serve others. In fact, the hymn is written to remind us that Jesus washed the disciple's feet, and we are to follow Jesus' example to love and serve others.

- Teach the children the refrain.

- Assign children to read one of the stanzas.

- **Say:** We can sing our prayer. As we sing and pray, think about the words. Thank God for filling us with love. Think about a person you can serve this week. We will sing the refrain, then one of you will read the stanza, then we will sing the refrain again.

- Continue until you finish reading all the stanzas.

- Dismiss children to their small groups.

Stay in Love

- Show the children the Bible verse.

- Encourage the children to read the Bible verse with you.

- **Ask:** What are some different ways that you can remain in Jesus' love?

- Encourage the children to share their ideas.

- **Say:** Prayer is one way we remain in Jesus' love. When we pray we talk to Jesus but we also listen. We often think of folding our hands together and bowing our heads when we pray. That's okay, but there are many other prayer positions. In fact, there is no wrong way to pray. Right now we are going to pray in several different ways. I will begin by saying a prayer position. Once everyone is in position, I will say a short prayer. We will repeat the process several times.

- Lead the children in prayer, giving the following prayer positions and the corresponding prayers.
    - o Head bowed and hands folded: Jesus Christ, we thank you that we can pray to you about anything.
    - o Hands raised high in the air: Jesus Christ, we thank you that we can pray when we are joyful and excited.
    - o Shoulders slumped, sad face: Jesus Christ, we thank you that you hear our prayers when we are sad.
    - o Kneeling: Jesus Christ, help us remember to talk with you often.
    - o Sports huddle: Jesus Christ, we thank you that we can pray to you wherever we are.
    - o Standing, hands spread out to the side: Jesus Christ, we thank you that we can pray to you about anything!
    - o Sitting: Jesus Christ, we thank you for hearing our prayers. Amen.

Prepare

✓ Write the Bible verse on a markerboard or a piece of mural paper, and place it where it can easily be seen. (Remain in my love. John 15:9b)

Small Groups

Divide the children into small groups. You may organize the groups around grade levels or around readers and nonreaders. Keep the groups small, with a maximum of twelve children in each group. You may need to have more than one group of each grade level.

Prepare

✓ Provide long strips of paper, pencils, baby food jars with lids, and bags of marbles.

✓ Write on a markerboard or a piece of mural paper: Love God and serve others.

Young Children

- **Say:** Jesus teaches us how to love God and serve others. We are to be Jesus' servants, loving God and others.

- **Ask:** What are some ways that you love God?

- Encourage children to share their answers.

- **Ask:** What are some ways that you serve others?

- Encourage children to share their answers.

- **Say:** I wonder if it was hard for Jesus to wash the disciples' dirty feet.

- **Ask:** What chores do you have at home? What chores do you have that are dirty jobs? What chores do you not like to do?

- **Say:** Sometimes we are to show God's love even when it's hard. When you do chores that are dirty jobs or chores that you don't like to do, you are showing God's love and serving others even when it is hard. When you help someone you don't like or don't know very well, you are loving and serving others when it is hard.

- **Ask:** When is it hard for you to serve?

- Give each child a strip of paper, a pencil, and a small jar.

- Tell the children to write "Love God and serve others" on their strip of paper.

- Have each child curl the strip of paper and place it in the jar so that the message is visible.

- Give each child a bag of marbles, and tell the children to take their jar home.

- **Say:** When you do something to love God or serve another person, add a marble to your jar. Try to fill up the jar!

- Stand in a circle. Encourage each child to complete this sentence prayer: Thank you God for . . .

- Remind the children to add a marble to their jar for showing their love of God!

Older Children

- **Say:** Today we have talked about remaining in love with God and serving others. We are to be Jesus' servants, loving God and others.
- **Say:** I wonder if it was hard for Jesus to wash the disciples' dirty feet.
- **Ask:** What chores do you have at home? What chores do you have that are dirty jobs? What chores do you not like to do?
- **Say:** Sometimes we are to show God's love even when it is hard. When you do something that you don't like to do, you are showing God's love and serving others even when it is hard. Judas was one of Jesus' disciples. He was a friend of Jesus, but Jesus knew that Judas would have him arrested, which would lead to Jesus' death.
- **Ask:** How do you think Jesus felt when he washed Judas' feet?
- **Say:** When you help someone you don't like or don't know very well, you are loving and serving others when it is hard.
- **Ask:** When is it hard for you to love or serve others?
- **Say:** When we remain in love with God, we want to serve others. We are going to do a service project. We are going to make thank-you cards for people who serve in our community.
- Let the children know who will receive the cards they make. Then give each child a piece of construction paper.
- Have each child fold the paper in half, bringing the short sides together, to make a card.
- Have each child place his or her card on a table with the fold facing right.
- Instruct the children to lay their left hands palm-down on the cards with their thumbs and index fingers resting barely over the fold. Make sure that the children's thumbs are slightly curled to male a half-heart shape.
- Encourage the children take turns using pencils to trace around each other's hands.
- Have the children cut out their handprints, beginning at the folded edge and not cutting the folded edges apart. Once cut out, ask the children to flip the card over so the fingers point down. The result should be a hand-shaped card that opens up to reveal a cutout heart shape between the thumbs and index fingers.
- Invite the children to write thank-you messages on their cards such as, "Thank you for serving God with your hands."
- Encourage the children to decorate their cards.
- **Say:** We too, can be servants of Jesus by loving God and loving and serving others.
- **Pray:** Loving Christ, you show us how to love God and how to love and serve others. Help us this week to be your servants. Help us this week to stay in love with God. Help us this week to show your love to others, even when it is hard. Amen.

Prepare

✓ Provide construction paper, pencils, scissors, crayons, and markers.

✓ Decide who will receive the cards the children will be creating. Possibilities include firefighters or police officers in your community, health care workers, and church staff or volunteers. Make arrangements for the cards to be delivered.

A Fun Way to Fold a Message

1. In the center of your piece of paper, write "Love God and love others."

2. Write or draw different ways you can show love to God and to others. If you'd like to, you can choose to write a letter to yourself.

3. When you're finished, lay the piece of paper in front of you so the square looks like a diamond and the writing is facing up.

4. Fold the bottom corner of the paper to the top corner to create a triangle. Crease well and then unfold.

5. Turn the paper to the other two corners of the diamond and repeat. Fold the bottom corner of the paper to the top corner to make a triangle. Crease well and then unfold. The creases you have made should form an X.

6. Put the diamond-shaped square in front of you. Fold the top corner down to the center fold line. Crease well.

7. Fold the bottom corner to the top of the page to meet the bottom edge of the triangle. Crease well.

8. Fold the right and left sides in, bringing them together in the center. Crease well. This should create the bottom point of your heart.

9. Turn the paper over.

10. Fold the top point down on each side. Crease well.

11. Fold the side point in on each side. Crease well.

12. Turn the paper over. Your message should now resemble a heart!

13. You can decorate your heart if you would like to.

Instructions from Jesus

Jesus is always with us.

Stay in love with God.

Love others.

Serve others.

5 Jesus the King

Objectives	Theme
The children will	Jesus wants to be King of our hearts.
• hear about Jesus' death.	
• explore ways that Jesus is King of our hearts.	**Bible Verse**
	Jesus the Nazarene, the king of the Jews. (John 19:19)

Focus for the Teacher

Jesus' death in the Gospel of John portrays Jesus as the King. Jesus prayed for others in the garden. Jesus proclaimed that he wanted to create God's kingdom in people's hearts. On the cross, Pilate posted a sign that read, "Jesus the Nazarene, the king of the Jews" (John 19:19), written in Aramaic, Latin, and Greek so everyone could read it and know that Jesus died for us.

Some children in your group will have experienced death. Young children do not understand the finality of death and often confuse words and language used to describe death. Older children can understand that death is final and tend to ask more questions about how the death happened.

As you talk with children about Jesus' death, keep these things in mind:

• Use clear, simple, and direct language. Graphic details are not necessary. Young children understand the emotions of Jesus' death. Older children will understand simple details of Jesus' death and become familiar with the people who participated in his death.

> We are believers. Jesus is King of our hearts.

• Be open and honest. It is fine to say that you don't completely understand why the people wanted to kill Jesus rather than follow him.

• All the children should be able to understand that Jesus is King and wants to live in their hearts.

• Assure children that Jesus loves us. Jesus was willing to die for us.

• Allow children's questions to guide your discussion.

• Be available to discuss the death of a pet or a loved one.

• Remind the children that even though the disciples and followers of Jesus were sad when he died, God had a surprise. Encourage them to come back next week to hear about the surprise.

Prior to this session, it will be helpful to read about Jesus' crucifixion and death in the Gospel of John 17–19 and in Chapter 5 of *John: The Gospel of Light and Life*. Note how the Gospel of John shows Jesus as King rather than portraying Jesus' human suffering. Note ways that we can celebrate with the children that Jesus is King!

Explore Interest Groups

Be sure that adult leaders are waiting when the first child arrives. Greet and welcome the children. Get the children involved in an activity that interests them and introduces the theme for the day's activities.

Who Is Jesus the Nazarene?

- Have the children study the map.
- **Ask:** Can you find Bethlehem? What happened in Bethlehem?
- Encourage children to recall the story of Jesus' birth.
- **Ask:** Can you find Jerusalem? What happened in Jerusalem?
- Encourage children to recall the story of Jesus' death.
- **Ask:** Can you find Nazareth?
- **Say:** Today's Bible verse is: Jesus the Nazarene, the king of the Jews, in John 19:19.
- Give each child a copy of Reproducible 5a: Jesus the Nazarene.
- Have the children look up the verse or passage in the Bible to answer the questions about Jesus the Nazarene.

Prepare

- ✓ Provide children's Bibles and a map of Palestine at the time of Jesus.
- ✓ Provide copies of **Reproducible 5a: Jesus the Nazarene**, found at the end of the lesson.

Spell It

- Divide children into groups of four.
- Have the groups spread out across the room so that each group has a large space on the floor to work on.
- Give each group a ball of yarn, a roll of tape, and a ruler.
- **Say:** Your task is to spell a word on the floor with your yarn. You can use tape to hold the yarn in place. Each letter in your word needs to be at least twelve inches high. Your word is INRI.
- Encourage each group to work together to spell the word with their yarn.
- Congratulate each group for completing the task.
- **Say:** INRI are the first letters of the four Latin words that mean "Jesus of Nazareth, king of the Jews." (It is called an acronym.) When Jesus was on the cross, this sign was nailed above Jesus' head. These words were also written in Aramaic and Greek so everyone could read them.

Prepare

- ✓ Provide a ball of yarn, a roll of tape, and a ruler for each group of four children.

Prepare

✓ Provide paper, crayons, and colored pencils.

Prepare

✓ This activity involves some messy elements, so think carefully about whether it's appropriate for your group. If it is, you may want to contact parents ahead of time to have their children wear clothes that won't be hurt by a spill.

✓ Provide flour, salt, cornstarch, water, bowls, spoons, measuring cups, toothpicks, waxed paper, watercolor paints, paintbrushes, plastic containers for water, and plastic table coverings or newspaper.

✓ Protect the work area with plastic table coverings or newspaper.

✓ Fill plastic containers one-third full with water and place them in the center of the table with the watercolor paints.

✓ *Tip*: If your time is limited, you may choose to make the clay before class.

Praying with Crayons

- **Say:** Before Jesus died, he was praying for us in the garden. There are many ways to pray. Some people like to pray while drawing.
- Give each child a piece of paper.
- Have each child use a crayon or marker to draw a free-form line on the paper that crosses over itself several times to create a large, loopy design.
- Invite the children to write *Jesus* in one of the central spaces.
- Add names of other people they want to pray for in the other spaces created by the line.
- Invite the children to use crayons or markers to decorate each space, thinking about the person's name in the space as they are decorating it.

Clay Cross

- Divide the class into groups of eight children each.
- Give each group a bowl and a spoon.
- Have each group make a batch of air-drying clay by mixing together one-fourth (1/4) cup each of flour, salt, cornstarch, and warm water. Add more water if the clay is too dry. If the clay is too wet, add more flour.
- Once the groups have made their clay, have them divide the clay into eight pieces, giving one piece to each group member.
- Give each child a piece of waxed paper to work on.
- Have children use their clay to make crosses.
- Give each child the option of using a toothpick to make a hole in the cross so it may be made into a necklace when dry.
- Invite the children to use watercolor paints to decorate their crosses.
- **Say:** This clay will be hard when it air-dries. If you have put a hole in your cross, you can make it into a necklace or an ornament. If you did not put a hole in your cross, you can set it on a shelf or table.
- **Ask:** What do you think of when you see a cross?
- **Say:** A cross can help us remember that Jesus died on a cross and that Jesus loves us.

Large Group

Bring all the children together to experience the Bible story. Use a bell to alert the children to the large-group time.

Crown for a King

- **Say:** I have two crowns, a king's crown and a crown of thorns.
- **Ask:** What crown would you want to wear? Why?
- **Say:** We do not have kings and queens in our country, but there are still kings and queens in other countries.
- **Ask:** What can you tell me about kings and queens?
- **Say:** A king or queen is the leader of a country. They wear a crown at ceremonies, to remind people that they are in charge of a country.
- **Ask:** How is this crown of thorns different from the king's crown? Who wore a crown of thorns? Why did Jesus wear a crown of thorns?
- **Say:** Jesus wore the crown of thorns before his crucifixion. The word crucifixion means that Jesus was nailed to a cross and died. The soldiers put the crown of thorns on Jesus' head to cause him pain and also to mock or tease him about being God's son. Jesus didn't want to be in charge of a country. Jesus wants to be King of our hearts.

Prepare

✓ Provide two crowns: a costume king's crown and a crown of thorns

We Are Believers of the King

- **Say:** When we believe something, that means we feel it is true. We have said today that we believe Jesus is King of our hearts.
- **Say:** The words of our hymns often tell what we believe about Jesus and what we believe about our relationship with Jesus. Let's read the words of the refrain together.
- Read the words together.
- **Ask:** What do these words tell us about Jesus, King of our hearts?
- **Say:** Jesus is King of our hearts. Jesus loves us so much that he was willing to die for us. Jesus wanted us to know that his love lasts forever. He wants all of us to adore him and tell others about his sacred name—to tell others who Jesus is.
- Teach the children to sing the refrain.
- **Say:** We are going to use the refrain as our prayer today. We will sing it several different times. Think about the words as you sing. Think about how Jesus is King of your heart.
- Sing the refrain three or four times.
- Dismiss the children to their small groups.

Prepare

✓ If you are not familiar with the hymn "Lift High the Cross," you can find it in many hymnals or online. You may also want to listen to the melody online.

✓ Provide a way for the children to access the words of the hymn.

Prepare

Jesus Is King

- **Say:** The last four weeks we have learned about Jesus.

- **Ask:** What do you remember about Jesus?

- **Say:** Today we are going to discover how Jesus is King. Jesus is both human and divine. Jesus lived on earth. His life was similar to our lives. He had parents, he experienced different feelings, he learned about many things, and he grew from a boy into a man. The first three Gospels—Matthew, Mark, and Luke—tell us about Jesus as a boy and as a man. In the Gospel of John, we learn how Jesus was divine. We learn how Jesus is God's son.

- **Say:** The other Gospels tell us about how Jesus suffered when people wanted to kill him. The Gospel of John tells us how Jesus was King. Jesus knew there was a reason for his death: it would fulfill his mission to be King of our hearts.

- **Ask:** I wonder, what does it mean to be King of our hearts?

- Encourage children to share their ideas.

- **Say:** Jesus wants to rule in our hearts. He wants us to love him. He wants us to love, to care, and to forgive one another.

- Give each child a copy of Reproducible 5b: Jesus Is King.

- **Say:** Let's learn more about Jesus, the King of our hearts. The leader will read a statement about Jesus. Everyone will respond after each statement with these words: Jesus is King of our hearts!

- Invite confident readers to help you read aloud the different statements.

- Continue reading one statement and responding until you finish all the statements.

- **Say:** This isn't the end of the story. You will have to wait until next week to find out what happened after Jesus died.

Prepare

King for All People

- Show the children the Bible verse.

- Encourage the children to read the Bible verse with you.

- **Say:** After Jesus was nailed to the cross, the sign—*Jesus the Nazarene, the king of the Jews*—was posted above Jesus' head. It was written in Aramaic, Latin, and Greek so everyone could read it. There were some people who thought Jesus was trying to be king of the Jewish people. Remember that Jesus didn't want to be a king of the Jewish people. He wants to be King of our hearts. Jesus wants us to share God's love with everyone.

- **Ask:** What are some ways that we can share with others our belief that Jesus is King of our hearts?

Small Groups

Divide the children into small groups. You may organize the groups around grade levels or around readers and nonreaders. Keep the groups small, with a maximum of twelve children in each group. You may need to have more than one group of each grade level.

Young Children

- **Ask:** What crown did Jesus wear?

- **Say:** Today, we are going to make a crown of thorns.

- Place plastic knives, small bowls of peanut butter, and bowls of broken pretzel pieces on a table. Give each child a sugar cookie.

- Have the children spread their cookie with peanut butter. Then, add pieces of the broken pretzel around the edge of the cookie to make the crown of thorns.

- **Say:** As you enjoy your snack, remember that we believe Jesus is King of our hearts. I wonder, What does that mean to you?

- Affirm children's thoughts. Remind them that Jesus' death is a mystery, bigger than we can understand. Throughout our lives we will be wondering what it means.

- **Pray:** Jesus, we thank you that you love us so much that you died for us. Show us how to live so that you are King of our hearts. Amen.

Prepare

- ✓ Provide sugar cookies, peanut butter, plastic knives, and broken pieces of pretzel.

- ✓ *Optional*: If a child has a peanut allergy, use a chocolate spread.

Older Children

- **Say:** When we believe something, that means we feel it is true. We have said today that we believe Jesus is King of our hearts.

- **Ask:** What does it mean for you to believe in Jesus?

- **Say:** In worship, we often say an affirmation. Affirmations are statements of what we believe about Jesus and our relationship with Jesus. Today we are going to write our own affirmations telling others what we believe about Jesus.

- Give each child a piece of paper.

- **Say:** Think for a minute. What would you tell others about Jesus? What do you believe about what Jesus does or has done for you personally, for your family, or for the world?

- Have each child complete the sentence: I believe . . .

- **Say:** We will use our affirmations as the closing prayer today. We will take turns reading our affirmations that tell about Jesus.

- Close the session by adding a prayer of your own to the children's affirmations.

Prepare

- ✓ Provide paper and pencils.

Jesus the Nazarene

Jesus grew up in the town of Nazareth, in the region of Galilee. Let's learn what happened to Jesus in Nazareth. Look up each verse or passage to answer the question about Jesus the Nazarene.

Luke 1:26-28   Mary and Joseph lived in Nazareth. What did the angel announce to Mary?

_____

Matthew 2:19-23   Why did Joseph, Mary, and Jesus move from Egypt back to Nazareth?

_____

Matthew 2:23   What name was Jesus called to identify him? Why?

_____

Luke 2:39-40   Who grew up in Nazareth?

_____

Luke 2:40   What happened to Jesus in Nazareth?

_____

Luke 4:16   What did Jesus do in the synagogue in Nazareth?

_____

Matthew 4:13-16   Why did Jesus move from Nazareth? Where did he move to?

_____

Jesus Is King

Jesus was in charge. He knew he was following God's plan. Jesus loves us so much that he was willing to die for us. He wanted us to know God's love is forever.

Jesus is King of our hearts!

After the last supper with his disciples, Jesus prayed for us. He prayed that we would stay safe and full of joy. Jesus prayed that we would stay in love with God.

Jesus is King of our hearts!

Judas brought some soldiers to arrest Jesus. They asked, "Are you Jesus the Nazarene?" Jesus said, "I Am."

Jesus is King of our hearts!

The leaders asked Jesus, "Are you the king of the Jews? Jesus said no. Jesus said he was King of our hearts. Jesus said he wanted to share God's love and truth.

Jesus is King of our hearts!

Pilate couldn't find that Jesus broke a law, but the people wanted Jesus to die. Pilate said, "Jesus will die." Jesus forgave the people.

Jesus is King of our hearts!

The soldiers teased Jesus. They made a crown of thorns for his head and dressed him in a purple robe. Jesus took their teasing.

Jesus is King of our hearts!

They nailed him to the cross to die. They put a sign above his head, "Jesus the Nazarene, the king of the Jews." It was written so everyone could read it. Jesus loves everyone!

Jesus is King of our hearts!

His mother was in the crowd watching. Jesus asked one of the disciples to take care of her.

Jesus is King of our hearts!

Jesus said, "It is complete. It is finished." Then he died. But it wasn't the end.

Jesus is King of our hearts!

6 Jesus Is Alive

Objectives

The children will
- learn about Jesus' resurrection.
- celebrate that we are Easter people.

Theme

On Easter, we celebrate Jesus' resurrection.

Bible Verse

"I've seen the Lord." (John 20:18)

Focus for the Teacher

Easter morning at dawn, Mary Magdalene went to the tomb in the garden where Jesus was buried. She was crying about the death of Jesus, her beloved friend and teacher. She looked in the tomb and it was empty. Troubled, she asked the two angels in the tomb where Jesus was. A person she thought was the gardener asked why she was crying. In surprise, Mary suddenly recognized that it was Jesus and after listening to him, left to tell the disciples.

As Christians, we believe that death is not the final word. We live as Easter people! We live with the promise of eternal life. We live knowing that our loved ones are in a wonderful place where there is amazing joy and where they are greeted by those they know and love. Our deep sadness and sorrow are transformed into joy. Our fears are transformed into peace and courage. We take on the responsibility to work within our families, our churches, and our communities to bring God's kingdom on earth.

The Resurrection story of Jesus in the Gospel of John is simple. Children can understand Mary's

> We are Easter people.

reaction to Jesus' death. Jesus had changed her life. Jesus had healed her, and she had followed him throughout Galilee. And now he was dead. Children can understand that when she didn't find him in the tomb, she was scared that someone had stolen his body. They also can understand her surprise and amazement when she realized Jesus was alive.

Children can claim these three Easter messages:

- God is powerful. On Easter, Jesus surprised everyone. Instead of being in the tomb, he was alive! God is the most powerful!

- Jesus promises that he is with us now and even after we die. Jesus, through the Holy Spirit, is always with us.

- We are living as Easter people when we share God's love with others.

Think about a time when someone you loved died. How did you feel? What did you think about the hope and promise of everlasting life that Jesus Christ offers?

Explore Interest Groups

Be sure that adult leaders are waiting when the first child arrives. Greet and welcome the children. Get the children involved in an activity that interests them and introduces the theme for the day's activities.

Alleluia Maracas

This activity is recommended for all children because they will use the maracas during the large-group time.

- **Say**: Today we are going to make musical instruments called maracas. We will use the maracas later during our large-group time.
- Give every child two plastic eggs and four plastic spoons.
- Have the children fill their eggs with the pony beads.
- Hold two plastic spoons facing each other.
- Use the washi tape to tape the bottom of two spoons together.
- Insert a filled plastic egg in between the spoons.
- Wrap the spoons and egg with washi tape to secure in place.
- Repeat to make the second maraca.

Prepare

- ✓ Provide plastic eggs, plastic spoons, small pony beads, washi tape, and scissors. The beads and tape can be purchased at a craft store. If possible, look for tape with symbols of spring or Easter or bright colors.
- ✓ Prior to class, put the pony beads in small plastic bowls.
- ✓ *Optional*: Use dried beans or rice to fill the eggs.

Easter Surprise

- Have the children sit at a table.
- **Say**: There are twelve Easter eggs hidden around the room.
- Have the children hunt the eggs. When a child finds an egg, ask them to bring it back to the table. Allow enough time for all the eggs to be found.
- **Say**: There is an important message hidden inside the eggs. Work together as a group to discover the message.
- Encourage the children to spell out Jesus is Alive. Give hints as necessary.
- **Say**: Easter is the day we celebrate that Jesus is alive!

Prepare

- ✓ Get twelve plastic eggs, strips of paper, and a marker.
- ✓ Prior to the session, write one letter of the phrase *Jesus is alive* on each strip of paper. Fold the strips of paper and stuff them into the eggs. Hide the eggs around the room.

Musical Review

- Have the children form a circle around the chairs.
- Start playing music and have the children begin walking around the circle.
- **Say**: When the music stops, find a chair.
- Stop the music and have each child find a seat.
- **Say**: You are not out of the game if you are left standing. Rather, you will tell us something that you remember about Jesus' life or a way that you can be a follower of Jesus.
- Invite the child left standing to share something they remember.

Prepare

- ✓ Provide a CD player and a CD of children's upbeat Christian music.
- ✓ Set up a circle of chairs, with the chairs facing to the outside of the circle, and using one fewer chair than the number of children playing.

- Remove a chair and start playing the music again, having the children walk around the circle.
- Stop the music and have each child find a seat. This time two people will be left standing.
- Invite each standing child to share something they remember. Encourage them to try to think of things that have not been shared already.
- Continue playing the game, removing one additional chair each round, until all the chairs are gone and all the children have spoken.

Prepare

✓ Write the phrase "Jesus' love is everlasting!" on a markerboard or a piece of mural paper, and place it where it can easily be seen.

✓ Cut 8½ x 11-inch paper in half lengthwise.

✓ Provide half-sheets of paper, tape, pencils, and scissors.

Never-Ending Promise

- Give each child a half-sheet of paper.
- Have each child fold their paper in half, bringing the long sides together, and then cut the paper along the fold line to make two long paper strips.
- Have each child tape their paper strips together to make one long strip, taping along the entire edge of the connection point on both sides.
- Encourage each child to bring the ends of their paper strip together, but just before forming a loop, have them make a half twist in one end.
- **Say:** You have just made a Mobius (Mo-bee-us) strip. A Mobius strip is special because it has no end; it only has one side. You can test this by drawing a line down the center of your Mobius strip. Place your pencil on your Mobius strip and begin drawing a line down the middle. Do not pick your pencil up until you return to the point where your line began.
- Encourage each child to draw a line down the center of their Mobius strip.
- **Say:** Notice that even though you never lifted your pencil, the line is on both sides of the paper! The surface of this Mobius strip is never-ending. Jesus' love is never-ending. It is everlasting. Jesus is always with us, even when we die.
- Encourage each child to write the phrase *Jesus' love is everlasting!* on their Mobius strip.
- **Ask:** What do you think would happen if we cut our Mobius strip in half?
- Have each child cut along the line they drew on the Mobius strip.
- **Ask:** What happened when you cut your Mobius strip in half? (It became one big circle.)
- **Say:** A circle is a good symbol that Jesus' love never ends. On Easter we celebrate that Jesus is alive and that his love is everlasting. Jesus will always be with us, even when we die. Jesus will always love us.

Large Group

Bring all the children together to experience the Bible story. Use a bell to alert the children to the large- IAMgroup time.

Sing Our Praise

- **Ask:** What are some words you hear at Easter?
- Encourage the children to share their ideas.
- **Say:** One word we use is *Alleluia*. That means we praise God that Jesus is alive!
- Provide access to the hymn.
- **Say:** We can celebrate that Jesus is alive! We can sing our praise!
- Teach the song and sing "Alleluia."

Alleluia! Jesus Is Alive!

- **Ask:** Who remembers what happened to Jesus last week?
- **Say:** Mary Magdalene was one of Jesus' friends. She was with Jesus and watched him die.
- **Ask:** How do you think she felt?
- **Say:** I can imagine that she was sad. In fact, I'm sure she was very sad.
- **Ask:** When have you been sad? What do you do when you are sad? How do you look when you are sad?
- Encourage children to show how their face, shoulders, and hands would look.
- Have the children get their Alleluia maracas.
- **Say:** Mary had a surprise when she went to Jesus' tomb. Let's hear what happened. Every time I say the word *Alleluia*, shake your maracas.
- Read the story from Reproducible 6a: Alleluia!
- **Ask:** How did Mary feel after she realized Jesus was alive? How do you think the look of Mary's face and body changed?
- Encourage children to show with their face, shoulders, and hands how Mary looked.
- Say: Remember that Alleluia means to praise God. We praise God that Jesus is alive!
- Have the group, stand up; shout, "Alleluia! Jesus is Alive!" and shake their maracas.

Prepare

- ✓ If you are not familiar with the hymn "Alleluia," you can find it in many hymnals or online. You may also want to listen to the melody online.
- ✓ Provide a way for the children to access the words of the hymn.
- ✓ *Optional*: Sing the song as a round, or add additional phrases.

Prepare

- ✓ Make a copy of **Reproducible 6a: Alleluia!** found at the end of the lesson.
- ✓ Children will need their Alleluia maracas.

Prepare

✓ Write the Bible verse on a markerboard or a piece of mural paper and place it where it can easily be seen. (I've seen the Lord. John 20:18)

Go! Tell Others!

- Show the children the Bible verse.

- Encourage the children to read the Bible verse with you.

- **Say:** Mary Magdalene couldn't believe that Jesus was alive. She went to tell the disciples, announcing, "I've seen the Lord." She wanted others to know that Jesus was alive. She wanted others to know that Jesus' love is everlasting—that it lasts forever. She wanted others to know that Jesus will always be with us.

- **Say:** Let's share God's good news! We will use different voices to tell others, "I've seen the Lord."

- Continue saying the Bible verse together, using each of the following types of voices: slow, fast, soft, bold, excited, loud.

We Are Easter People!

- **Say:** Jesus is alive! That means Jesus is always with us now and even after we die. We live as Easter people knowing that Jesus will never stop loving us. We live as Easter people sharing God's love with others. Let's do a cheer to celebrate that we are Easter people.

- Divide the children into six groups. Have each group move to a different area around the room.

- **Say:** Our cheer is going to be, "We are Easter people! Yes, we are! How about you?"

- Encourage the children to practice with you.

- **Say:** I will choose one group to begin. That group will do a quick huddle to decide which group they will pass the cheer to, then they will say the cheer. When they say "How about you?" they will point to the group they have chosen. That group will do a quick huddle to decide which group they will pass the cheer to, then they will say the cheer. In this way we will pass the cheer around the room.

- Choose a group to begin the cheer.

- Encourage the children to pass the cheer around the room, making sure every group is included.

- To end the cheer, say, "Last time! This time, everybody answers."

- Dismiss children to their small groups.

Small Groups

Divide the children into small groups. You may organize the groups around grade levels or around readers and nonreaders. Keep the groups small, with a maximum of twelve children in each group. You may need to have more than one group of each grade level.

Young Children

- **Say:** Since this is the last week of our study on Jesus, you are going to make a game to play at home that will remind you about what we have discussed.

- **Ask:** What does it mean for us to be children of the light? (Hold up the corresponding craft stick that you made.)

- Continue until you review all six phrases.

- Give each child six craft sticks and a copy of Reproducible 6b: We Are….

- Have each child cut out the six phrases and glue them on the craft sticks.

- Give each child an envelope where they can put their craft sticks.

- Invite the children to decorate their envelopes.

- **Say:** To play today's game, take one stick from your envelope. Read the phrase on the stick. Share one way that you can live as the description on your stick.

- Divide the children into small groups and allow them to play the game.

- When the game ends, give one of the sticks you made to six different children in your group.

- **Say:** We are going to stand in a circle and pray together. We can pray with our eyes open. If I've given you a stick, read the phrase on it and ask God to help you live as the description on your stick.

- Have the six children pray.

- **Say:** And all God's people said: (together) Amen.

Prepare

- ✓ Provide copies of **Reproducible 6b: We Are…** found at the end of the lesson.

- ✓ Provide construction paper, craft sticks, scissors, glue sticks, envelopes, and crayons.

- ✓ *Tip*: Prior to class, glue each of the six phrases from We Are…on six craft sticks.

- ✓ *Optional*: Send a note home to the parents encouraging them to choose one or more sticks at dinner time or family devotion time and use the sticks to discuss ways their family is living as followers of Jesus.

Prepare

✓ Provide a copy of **Reproducible 6b: We Are...** found at the end of the lesson.

✓ Cut the reproducible into strips of paper as indicated. Place the strips in a basket.

✓ *Optional*: Record a video of each group's commercial and send to the children to watch at home.

Older Children

- **Say:** This is our last week. We have been learning about Jesus and how we are to be followers of Jesus. Remember that:
  o Jesus is the light for all people. We are children of the light.
  o Jesus cares for all of us. We are compassionate kids, showing our care for others.
  o Jesus is the way, the truth, and the life. We are followers of the Way.
  o Jesus gives us instructions to be servants of Christ, remaining in love with God and loving others.
  o Jesus is King of our hearts. We believe in Jesus.
  o Jesus is alive! We are Easter people.

- Divide the children into six groups.

- Have each small group draw a slip of paper from the basket.

- **Say:** Read your slip of paper, and as a group create a commercial to share with the others.

- Encourage the children and help as needed as they plan their commercial. Allow enough time for all groups to make a plan.

- **Say:** Let's come back together and share our commercials.

- Invite each group to share their commercial.

- **Say:** Now we remember all the things we have learned during the last six weeks.

- Have the children stand in a circle.

- **Say:** We can pray with our eyes open. We are going around the circle and give everyone a chance to pray. If you would rather not pray, you can squeeze the person's hand to pass. Let us pray.

- **Say:** And all God's people said: (together) Amen.

Alleluia!

Shake your Alleluia maracas every time the word "Alleluia!" is said.

It was early Easter morning. Alleluia!

Mary Magdalene was sad. Her friend, Jesus, was dead.

Jesus had healed her. Alleluia!

Jesus had been her teacher. Alleluia!

Mary's life was better after she met Jesus. In fact, it was a lot better! Alleluia!

Mary walked to the tomb where Jesus was buried.

Jesus' body wasn't there. Did someone steal it?

Mary was angry. She was feeling hopeless and didn't know what to do.

She was sad and crying so hard that she didn't recognize Jesus.

Then Jesus called her by name. He said, "Mary." Alleluia!

Mary realized that Jesus was alive! Alleluia! Alleluia!

Jesus was still with her! Alleluia!

Mary knew that Jesus was alive! Alleluia!

Mary knew that Jesus would always be with her. Alleluia!

Alleluia! Alleluia! Alleluia!

–Based on John 20:1-23

We Are...

Children of the Light

Compassionate Kids

Followers of the Way

Servants of Christ loving God and others

Believers—Jesus is the King of our hearts

Easter People

www.ingramcontent.com/pod-product-compliance
Lightning Source LLC
Chambersburg PA
CBHW080609090426

42735CB00017B/3376